PLAY IT AS IT LIES

Also by Norman Thelwell

Angels on Horseback
Thelwell Country
A Place of Your Own
Thelwell in Orbit
A Leg at Each Corner
Top Dog
Thelwell's Riding Academy
Up the Garden Path
The Compleat Tangler
Thelwell's Book of Leisure
This Desirable Plot
The Effluent Society
Penelope
Three Sheets in the Wind
Belt Up
Thelwell Goes West
Thelwell's Brat Race
A Plank Bridge by a Pool
Thelwell's Gymkhana
Thelwell's Pony Cavalcade
A Millstone Round My Neck
Some Damn Fool's Signed the Rubens Again
Thelwell's Magnificat
Thelwell's Sporting Prints
Wrestling with a Pencil
Thelwell's Pony Panorama

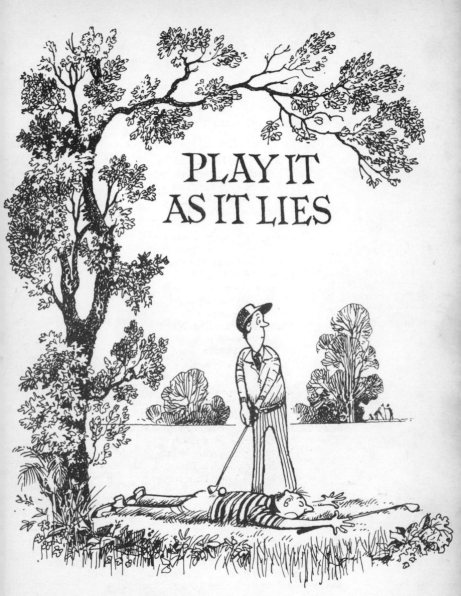

PLAY IT
AS IT LIES

A METHUEN PAPERBACK

A Methuen Paperback

First published in Great Britain 1987
by Methuen London Ltd
This paperback edition published in 1988
by Methuen London
Michelin House,
81 Fulham Road,
London SW3 6RB
© 1987 Norman Thelwell

Made and printed in Great Britain
by Richard Clay Ltd, Bungay, Suffolk

British Library Cataloguing in Publication Data

Thelwell, *1923*–
Play it as it lies.
1. English humorous cartoons –
Collections from individual artists
I. Title
741.5′942

ISBN 0–413–19240–7

CONTENTS

THE TRUTH ABOUT GOLF

Golf is without doubt
the easiest ball game known to man.

If you can swat a fly with a rolled-up newspaper . . .

. . . or knock the head off a daisy with a stick –
you can play golf.

The game requires no great physical strength . . .

. . . or athletic ability.

It can be taken up at any age . . .

. . . and provide a lifetime of enjoyment for all.

Some people take up golf
in order to make business contacts —

— others to enjoy the fresh air and exercise.

Some see it as a means of escape
from domestic responsibilities –

– to others it is an aid to social climbing.

Whatever his motivation, however, one thing is certain —
the golfer is a happy man . . .

. . . provided, of course,
that he does not start reading about how to do it –

– or seeking the advice of experts.

TALKING GOLF

It is important that the aspiring golfer
learns the meaning of certain golfing terms,
so that he can understand what his fellow sportsmen
are saying to him.

This man is 'hitting three off the tee'.

This one is 'blasting out of a bunker'.

This is known as 'a dog leg' (or 'casual water').

It is best dealt with by the 'pitch and run shot'.

Here is 'a downhill lie'.

And a 'golfing widow'.

This is 'a full member'.

This player is 'taking a free drop'.

They are both now 'pin high'.

And taking 'the nap of the green'.

This sportsman is 'playing through the green'.

This one is 'playing around'.

'Bounce' is an integral part of the game . . .

. . . so is 'the rub of the green'.

Hitting the ball as far as you can up the fairway
is known as 'the long game'.

Putting out on the green is called 'the short game'.

'Direction post'.

RULES AND ETIQUETTE

It is essential that you address your ball with care
before driving off — so that you can recognise it at all times.

Failure to identify your own ball
may lead to frayed tempers –

– or flouting of the rules of golf.

It is unforgivable to use gamesmanship on the golf course –
either by ill-timed noises . . .

... or questionable actions.

Dress and equipment should be neat and practical.

Eccentric clothing may tend to interfere with play.

Do not attempt
to replace your divots
on the teeing ground
otherwise the green sward
may become loose
and powdery.

Once on the fairway, however, all divots must be firmly replaced
to discourage scavenging birds.

You are not permitted to accept physical assistance
when playing your shots . . .

. . . or to be sheltered from the elements when doing so.

You may not move earth or rocks to improve your stance . . .

. . . and wilful destruction of growing vegetation
is against the rules.

Golf is a game of trust and you will often
find yourself alone with your conscience.

Remember that if you move your ball by accident
you are deemed to have played another shot.

You are required to fill in
any hollows you have made in bunkers.

Hand warmers are legal
but must not be used to warm anything else.

You may not use mechanical gadgets
to assess wind speed and direction . . .

. . . but you are permitted
to toss a little grass into the air.

It is your right to declare
your ball unplayable at any time
– provided that your declaration
can be heard by everyone concerned.

GOLF IN THE GARDEN

'It went straight down the waste disposal unit.'

LITTLE NIPPER SAND PIT

GOLF IN THE HOME

'That's where the pain gets me, doc.'

GOLF IN THE OFFICE

'Sometimes I think you love your golf
more than you love me, Mr Pilkington.'

'How do you like being on the board of directors, Wilkins?'

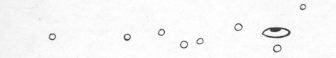

'Don't you *ever* relax, J.B.?'

'Who's responsible for this shoddy thing?'

'What the hell's going on on the shop floor?'

'I said, can I have my ball back, please?'

'When did you start feeling
that people were ignoring you?'

LADIES' GAME

'Would you help me with my zipper please?'

'I've got a hole in one.'

'Hand me a number eight iron.'

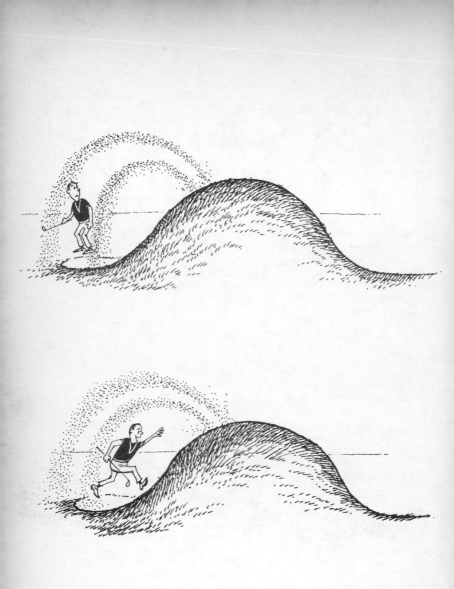

'FORE!'

'I notice it's always *my* ball you accidentally drive over.'

'We found her ball
but now she's lost an earring.'

'We found her earring
then bang went her beads.'

A NATURAL HISTORY FOR GOLFERS

Most golfers spend many hours communing with nature.
Here is a simple guide to make it even more enjoyable.

FLORA

Semi-rough. All grasses, weeds and wild
flowers from about four to eight inches in
height belong to the genus semi-rough. Any
players slicing into it can usually be seen
giving thanks for a narrow escape.

Deep Rough. A very varied family of
plants up to five and more feet in height.
Golfers can frequently be heard calling
them by a wide variety of incorrect names.

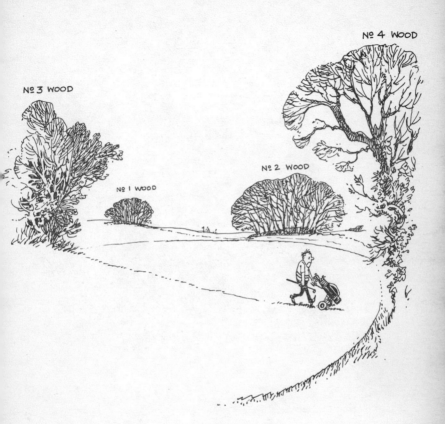

No 4 WOOD

No 3 WOOD

No 2 WOOD

No 1 WOOD

Woods. Nos. 1, 2, 3 and 4 woods are the names given to collections of trees which have a strange attraction for golf balls. Most golfers find that three woods are quite enough.

Deciduous Woods. Drop all their leaves in
the autumn so that any ball that comes to
rest in them is lost for six months at least.

Coniferous Woods. Keep their leaves
firmly in place and make it so dark that it
is impossible to find a ball at any time of
the year.

FAUNA

Rabbits. The cuddly little creatures that can be seen digging holes all over the countryside.

Tigers. Almost never seen in the woods but can frequently be spotted moving very fast down the fairway.

Ferrets. A common sight on the golf course – chipping off the fairway onto the putting green.

Game. Usually erupts suddenly from the woods.

Par. A young salmon which you may be lucky enough to spot if you have sliced into a river.

Birdie. A tiny creature that sings its heart out to charm the nature lover.

Eagle. Rarely seen except on Scottish courses.

Albatross. If you ever hit one of these you will remember it for the rest of your life.

Woodpecker. Can be seen and heard on most courses rapping away on the trees.

USEFUL TIPS

When big money is at stake, top golfers find it
well worth while to employ professional caddies.

A visor is very helpful
when trying to follow the flight of your ball.

It is courteous to watch the flight
of your opponent's ball also —
so that you can tell him where it landed.

Never park your golf trolley in inconvenient places —

– or drive your golf buggy without due care and attention.

Remember that you are allowed to abandon a game
if there is a danger of being struck by lightning . . .

. . . or if a player becomes seriously indisposed.

Do not get depressed
if you are not playing your best game . . .

. . . and *never* take your spite out
on other people – after all –

– golf is only a game.